Textbook
1A

Maths — No Problem!

Singapore Maths
English National Curriculum 2014

Consultant and Author
Dr. Yeap Ban Har

UK Consultant
Dr. Anne Hermanson

Authors
Dr. Foong Pui Yee
Chang Suo Hui
Lim Li Gek Pearlyn
Wong Oon Hua

shinglee

Published by Maths — No Problem!
Copyright © 2016 by Maths — No Problem!

Printed in the United Kingdom
First Printing, 2014
Reprinted in 2014, twice in 2015 and twice in 2016

ISBN 978-1-910504-00-0

Maths — No Problem!
Dowding House, Coach & Horses Passage
Tunbridge Wells, UK TN2 5NP
www.mathsnoproblem.co.uk

Acknowledgements

This Maths — No Problem! series, adapted from the New Syllabus
Primary Mathematics series, is published in collaboration with
Shing Lee Publishers. Pte Ltd.

Design and Illustration by Kin

Preface

Maths — No Problem! is a comprehensive series that adopts a spiral design with carefully built-up mathematical concepts and processes adapted from the maths mastery approaches used in Singapore. The Concrete-Pictorial-Abstract (C-P-A) approach forms an integral part of the learning process through the materials developed for this series.

Maths — No Problem! incorporates the use of concrete aids and manipulatives, problem-solving and group work.

In Maths — No Problem! Primary 1, these features are exemplified throughout the chapters:

Chapter Opener

Familiar events or occurrences that serve as an introduction for pupils.

In Focus

Includes questions related to various lesson objectives as an introductory activity for pupils.

Let's Learn

Introduces new concepts through a C-P-A approach with the use of engaging pictures and manipulatives. Guided examples are provided for reinforcement.

Activity Time

Provides pupils with opportunities to work as individuals or in small groups to explore mathematical concepts or to play games.

Guided Practice

Comprises questions for further consolidation and for the immediate evaluation of pupils' learning.

If 3 balloons fly off, how many balloons remain?

Mind Workout

Challenging non-routine questions for pupils to apply relevant heuristics and to develop higher-order thinking skills.

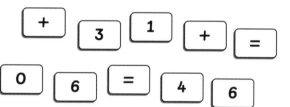

Maths Journal

Provides pupils with opportunities to show their understanding of the mathematical concepts learnt.

Self Check

Allows pupils to assess their own learning after each chapter.

Self Check

I know how to...

☐ Count to 10.
☐ Read and write numbers from 0 to 10.
☐ Compare and order numbers from 0 to 10.

Contents

Chapter 1	Numbers to 10	Page
1	Counting to 10	2
2	Counting Objects to 10	4
3	Writing to 10	7
4	Counting to Zero	10
5	Comparing Numbers of Objects	13
6	Ordering Numbers	17
7	Comparing Numbers	20

Chapter 2	Number Bonds	
1	Making Number Bonds	26
2	Making Number Stories	29

Chapter 3	Addition Within 10	Page
1	Add by Using Number Bonds	34
2	Add by Counting On	37
3	Completing Number Sentences	40
4	Making Addition Stories	42
5	Solving Picture Problems	45

Chapter 4	Subtraction Within 10	
1	Subtract by Crossing Out	50
2	Subtract by Using Number Bonds	52
3	Subtract by Counting Back	54
4	Making Subtraction Stories	56
5	Solving Picture Problems	58
6	Addition and Subtraction	60

Chapter 5	**Positions**	**Page**
1	Naming Positions	64
2	Naming Positions in Queues	67
3	Naming Left and Right Positions	69

Chapter 6	**Numbers to 20**	
1	Counting to 20	74
2	Writing to 20	78
3	Comparing Numbers	80
4	Ordering Numbers	84
5	Number Patterns	87

Chapter 7	**Addition and Subtraction Within 20**	
1	Add by Counting On	92
2	Add by Making 10	94
3	Add by Adding Ones	98
4	Subtract by Counting Back	100
5	Subtract by Subtracting Ones	102
6	Subtract from 10	104
7	Addition and Subtraction Facts	106

Chapter 8	Shapes and Patterns	Page
1	Recognising Solids	110
2	Recognising Shapes	113
3	Grouping Shapes	118
4	Making Patterns	121

Chapter 9	Length and Height	
1	Comparing Height and Length	126
2	Measuring Length Using Things	129
3	Measuring Height and Length Using Body Parts	131
4	Measuring Height and Length Using a Ruler	134

How many balls
are there?

Chapter 1
Numbers to 10

Counting to 10

In Focus

| 7 | 3 | 4 | 2 | 6 | 8 | 9 | 10 | 1 | |

Arrange the numbers in order.
What is the missing number?

There is a missing number.

Let's Learn

1

Count on from 1.

1, 2, 3, 4, 5

2

Count on from 4.

4, 5, 6, 7, 8, 9, 10

3

Count back from 10.

10, 9, 8, 7, 6, 5, 4

4

Count back from 6.

6, 5, 4, 3, 2, 1

Guided Practice

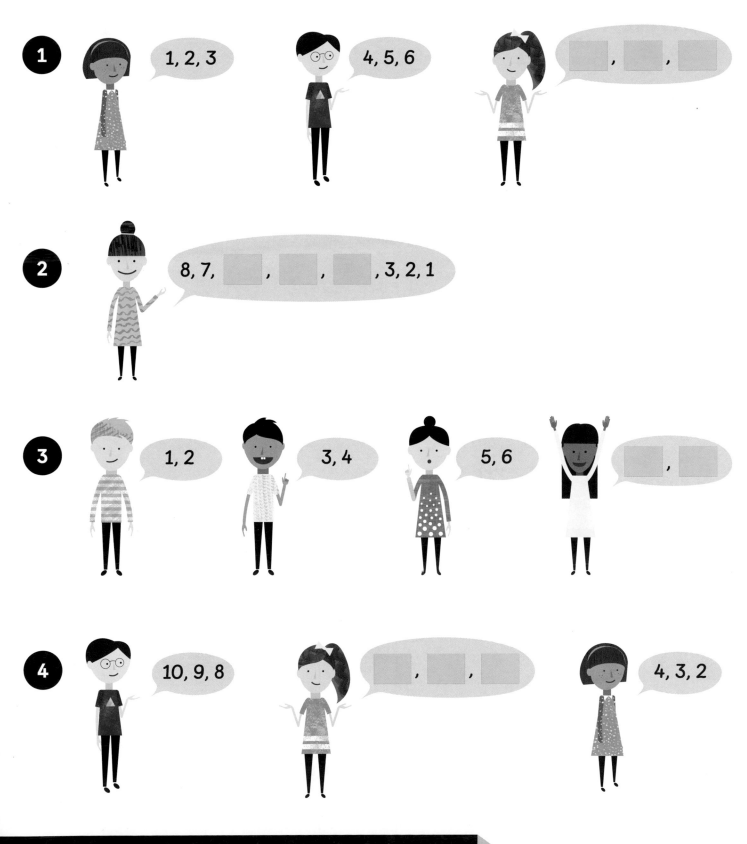

1 1, 2, 3   4, 5, 6   ☐, ☐, ☐

2 8, 7, ☐, ☐, ☐, 3, 2, 1

3 1, 2   3, 4   5, 6   ☐, ☐

4 10, 9, 8   ☐, ☐, ☐   4, 3, 2

Complete Worksheet **1** – Page **1 – 4**

Counting Objects to 10

In Focus

Count.
How many are there?

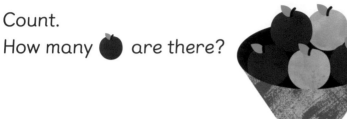

Show the numbers on 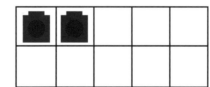 using .

Let's Learn

1

2

3

4

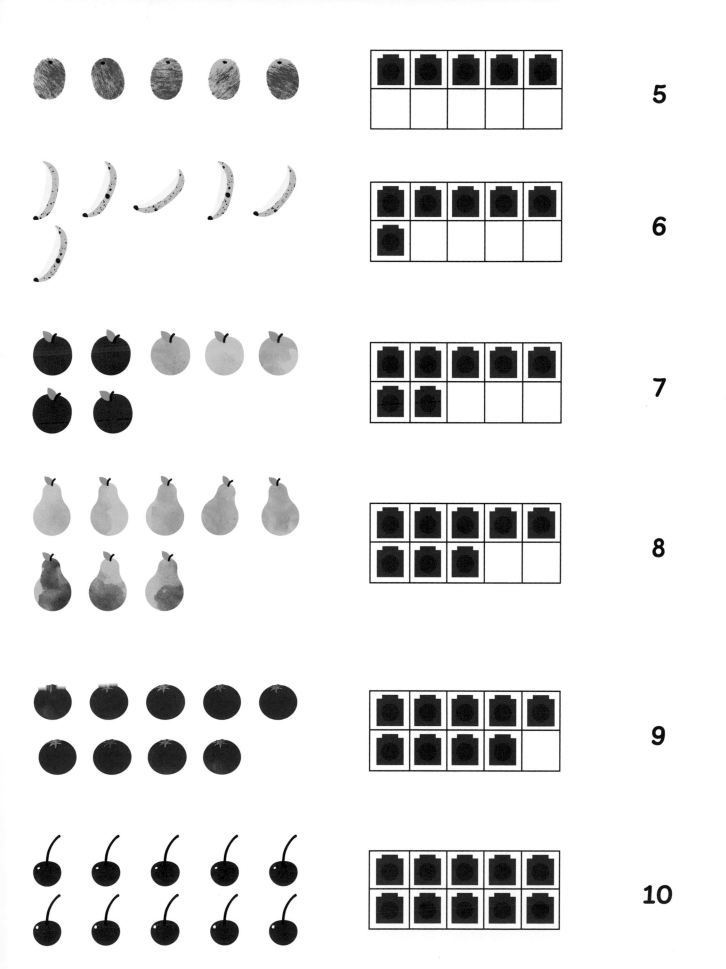

5

6

7

8

9

10

Work in groups.

1. Shake the box.

2. Guess how many 🫘 there are in the box.

3. Open the box and count the number of 🫘.

4. Show the number using ⬛ and ▭.

5. Show the number using 🂠 and 🂠.

What you need:

Guided Practice

Count.

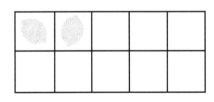

1, 2

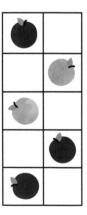

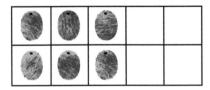

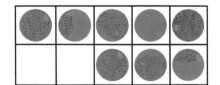

Complete Worksheet **2** – Page **5 - 8**

Writing to 10

In Focus

Count.
How many balls are there?

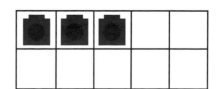

Show the numbers on  using ▦.

Let's Learn

Count the things in the cupboard.

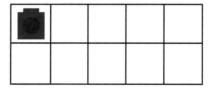   1
one

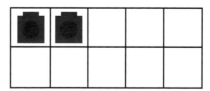   2
two

   3
three

  **4**
four

 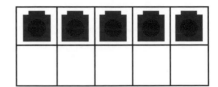 **5**
five

  **6**
six

 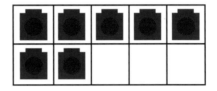 **7**
seven

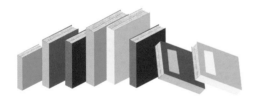 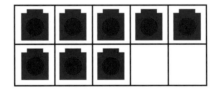 **8**
eight

 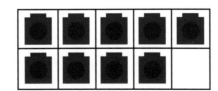 **9**
nine

 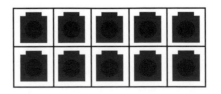 **10**
ten

Guided Practice

1 Count the eggs and muffins.

Show the number on ▦ using ⬛.

Pick out the correct number ⬚2 and word ⬚two.

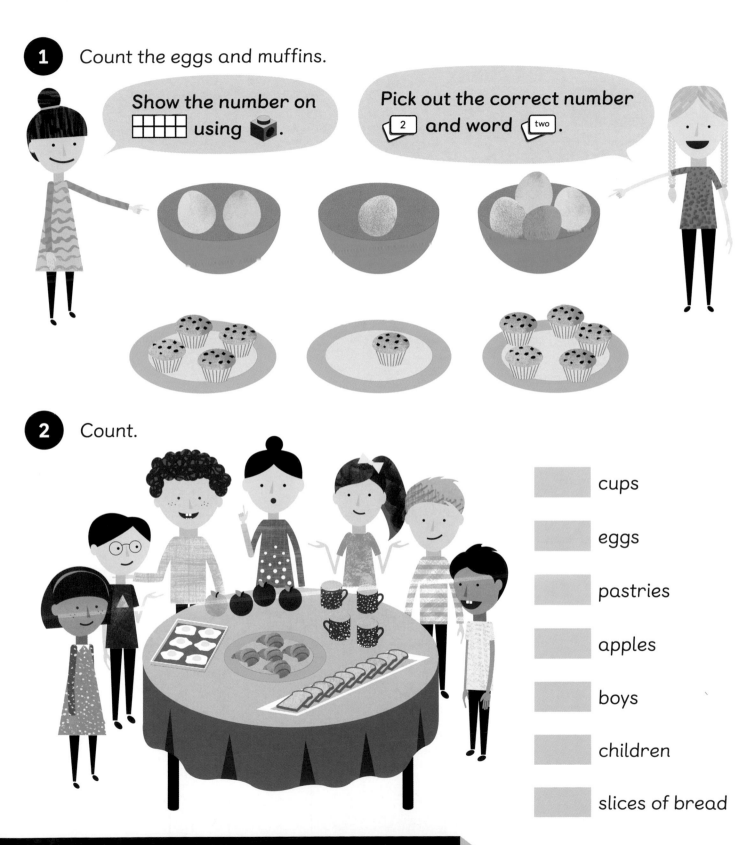

2 Count.

cups

eggs

pastries

apples

boys

children

slices of bread

Complete Worksheet **3** – Page **9 – 12**

Counting to Zero

In Focus

What happens when a tiger comes?

Let's Learn

There are 3 monkeys.

There are 2 monkeys.

There is 1 monkey.

There are no monkeys.

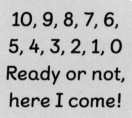

10, 9, 8, 7, 6, 5, 4, 3, 2, 1, 0
Ready or not, here I come!

Hide and seek!

0

zero

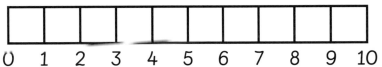

① Pick a stick.

② Say the number.

③ Shade the number of 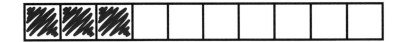 in ⬚⬚⬚⬚⬚⬚⬚⬚⬚⬚⬚ .
    0 1 2 3 4 5 6 7 8 9 10

④ Count up from the number to 10.

⑤ Count down from the number to 0.

Three

3, 2, 1, 0   3, 4, 5, 6, 7, 8, 9, 10

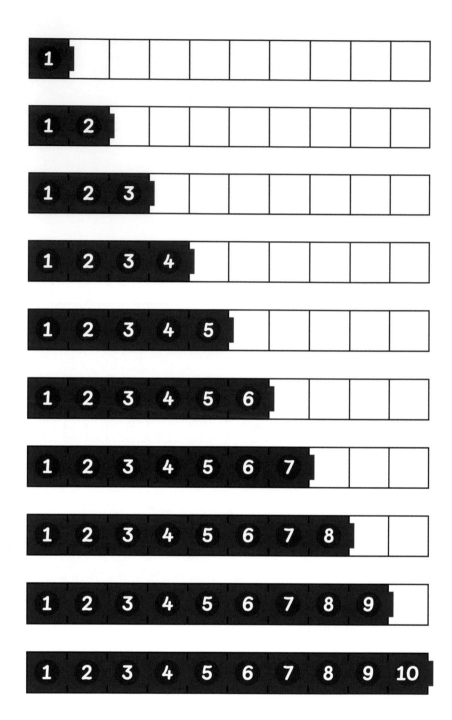

Count aloud from 1 to 10.

Count back from 10 to 1.

Complete Worksheet 4 – Page 13

Comparing Numbers of Objects

In Focus

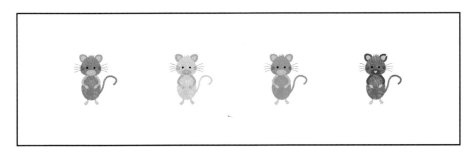

How can we tell?

Are there more or ?

Are there more or ?

Let's Learn

1

I can match them.

There are 4 rabbits.
There are 4 mice.
There are **as many** rabbits **as** mice.
The number of rabbits is **equal to** the number of mice.

2

5 is more than 4.

4 is less than 5.

There are 4 rabbits.
There are 5 squirrels.
There are more squirrels than rabbits.
There are fewer rabbits than squirrels.

Work in pairs.

What you need:

Group A

Group B

Place ■ in Group A and Group B to show that:

①   Group A has more ■ than Group B.

②   Group A has fewer ■ than Group B.

③   Group A has as many ■ as Group B.

④   The number of ■ in Group B is equal to the number of ■ in Group A.

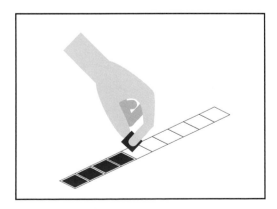

Guided Practice

1 Which group has more things?

Group A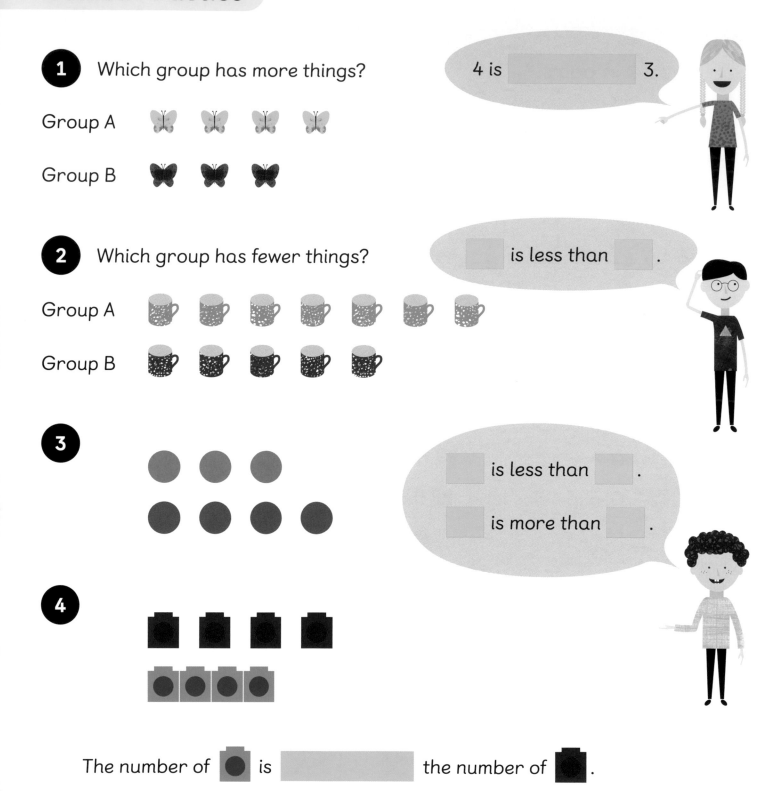

Group B

4 is _____ 3.

2 Which group has fewer things?

Group A

Group B

_____ is less than _____.

3

_____ is less than _____.

_____ is more than _____.

4

The number of ⬤ is _____ the number of ⬛ .

Complete Worksheet **5** – Page **14 - 17**

Ordering Numbers

In Focus

How do we know?

Compare the number of snacks.
Which plate has the most snacks?

Let's Learn

1 There are 3 cupcakes.

There are 5 cookies.

5 is more than 3.

3 is less than 5.

| 1 | 2 | **3** | 4 | **5** | 6 | 7 | 8 | 9 | 10 |

2 There are 3 cupcakes.

There are 5 cookies.

There are 7 doughnuts.

Which number is more than the others?
Which number is less than the others?

| 1 | 2 | **3** | 4 | **5** | 6 | **7** | 8 | 9 | 10 |

7 is more than 5.
7 is more than 3.
7 is the **greatest**.

3 is less than 7.
3 is less than 5.
3 is the **smallest**.

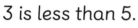

| 7 | 5 | 3 |

| 3 | 5 | 7 |

I can arrange the numbers from the greatest to the smallest.

I can arrange the numbers from the smallest to the greatest.

Guided Practice

 Which number is greater?

(a)
| 2 | 9 |

(b)
| 6 | 5 |

2 Which number is the smallest?

| 4 | 1 | 3 |

 Arrange the numbers in order.

(a) Start with the greatest.

2,   **7,**   **5**

⬜ ,   ⬜ ,   ⬜

greatest ⟶ smallest

(b) Start with the smallest.

9,   **10,**   **4**

⬜ ,   ⬜ ,   ⬜

smallest ⟶ greatest

Complete Worksheet 6 – Page 18 – 20

Comparing Numbers

What number does this show?
What is 1 more than it?
What is 1 less than it?

Let's Learn

1   This shows 6.

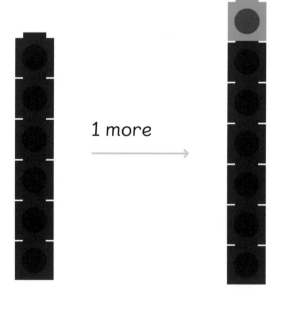

1 more

7 is 1 more than 6.
7 is more than 6.

2 This shows 6.

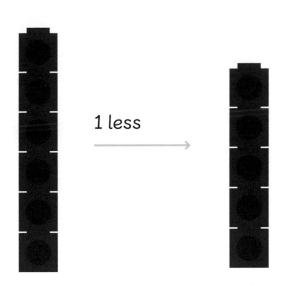

1 less

5 is 1 less than 6.
5 is less than 6.

3 Let's compare 5, 6 and 7.

5

6

7

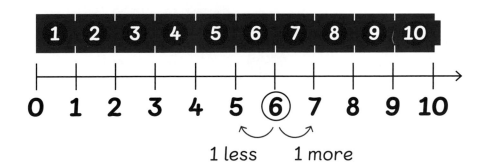

1 less   1 more

Work in pairs.

What you need:

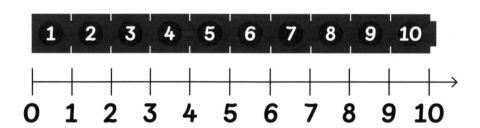

① Show your partner some ⬛. Use fewer than 10.

② Your partner tells you a number that is 1 more than the one you show.

③ You tell your partner a number that is 1 less than the one you show.

④ Repeat ① to ③.

Guided Practice

```
1  2  3  4  5  6  7  8  9  10
```

```
0  1  2  3  4  5  6  7  8  9  10
```

1 This shows 4.

[ ] is 1 less than 4.

[ ] is 1 more than 4.

2 [ ] is less than 8.

[ ] is 1 less than 8.

3 [ ] is more than 8.

[ ] is 1 more than 8.

Complete Worksheet 7 – Page **21 – 22**

Look for these numbers written as words in the puzzle.

1	2	3	4	5	6	7	8	9	10

i	s	h	b	c	q	s	i	n	g
e	i	g	h	t	r	t	a	f	a
j	x	d	d	w	a	s	p	o	s
k	e	l	e	o	n	e	p	o	t
a	z	m	f	b	c	v	l	m	h
o	y	g	f	i	v	e	e	x	r
v	m	h	o	o	p	n	i	n	e
j	x	i	u	t	u	n	a	n	e
a	z	e	r	o	p	o	c	a	t
k	l	m	a	n	q	r	s	a	m

Which number from 1 to 10 is not in the puzzle?

Maths Journal

Draw pictures to match each card.

| five apples | 8 balls | two cakes |

Sam's Journal

3 birds

I know how to...

☐ count to 10.

☐ read and write numbers from 0 to 10.

☐ compare and order numbers from 0 to 10.

Self Check

Chapter 2
Number Bonds

Making Number Bonds

How many cupcakes are there on each plate?
Is there another way to put the cupcakes on the two plates?

Let's Learn

1 Put 5 cupcakes on two plates.

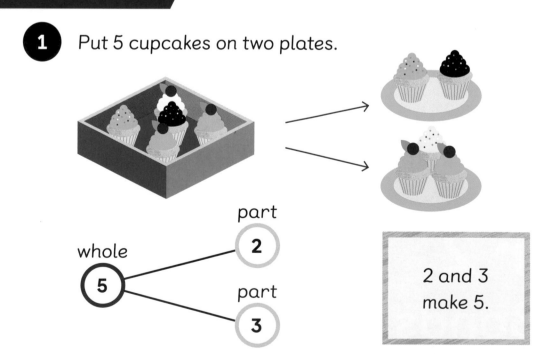

part

whole

5

2

part

3

2 and 3
make 5.

This is a **number bond**.

2 There are other ways to make 5.

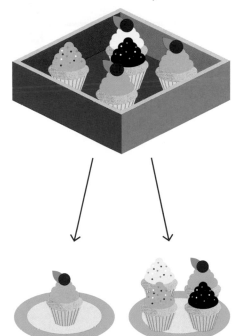

whole

5

part **1**   **4** part

1 and 4
make 5.

3

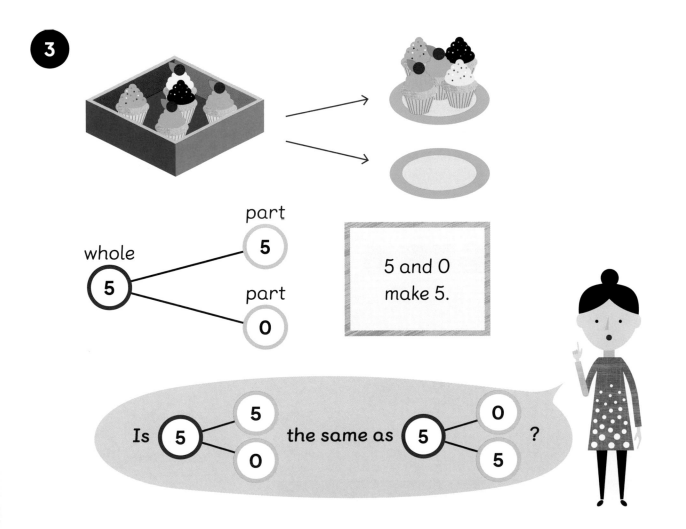

whole
5

part
5

part
0

5 and 0
make 5.

Is **5** — 5 / 0 the same as **5** — 0 / 5 ?

Work in groups of 4.

① Make number bonds of 6.

② Put  on the to show different ways to make 6.

③ Take turns to make number bonds for different numbers.

What you need:

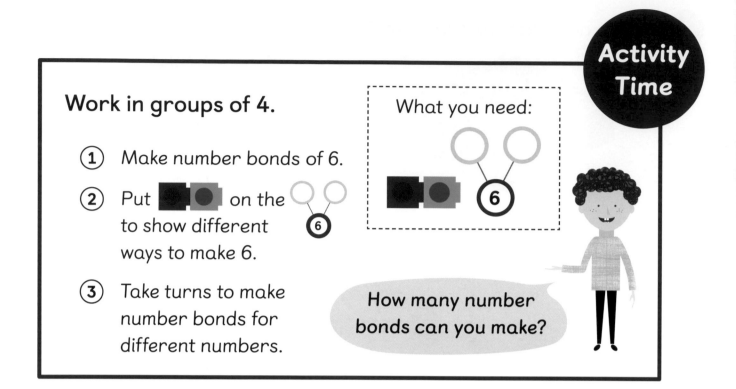

How many number bonds can you make?

Guided Practice

Complete the number bonds.

(a)

and make 7.

whole ⑦ part / part

(b)

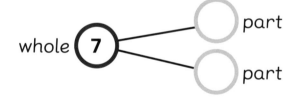

2 and 8 make .

whole ◯ ② part / ⑧ part

(c)

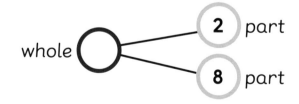

4 and make 10.

whole ⑩

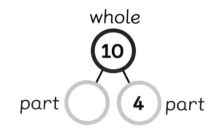

part ◯ ④ part

Complete Worksheet **1** – Page **27 - 30**

Making Number Stories

In Focus

How are the slices of cake different?

Let's Learn

We can make number stories.

There are 4 slices of cake.
3 slices have cherries.
1 slice has no cherry.

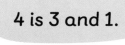

4 is 3 and 1.

There are 4 slices of cake.
2 slices are pink.
2 slices are yellow.

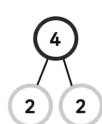

4 is 2 and 2.

Work in pairs.

What you need:

① Tell a number story.

② Get your partner to use 🍎 and 🔵 to show the number story.

9 is 7 and 2.

There are
9 pieces of fruit.
7 of them are oranges.
2 of them are apples.

③ Take turns to tell number stories with different numbers.

Guided Practice

Make number stories.

 1

There are 9 kittens.

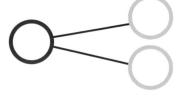 kittens are grey.

kittens are brown.

There are ☐ children.

There are ☐ boys.

There are ☐ girls.

☐ children wear glasses.

☐ children do not wear glasses.

Complete Worksheet **2** · Page **31 – 33**

Mind Workout

There are 8 ⬤ on the table.

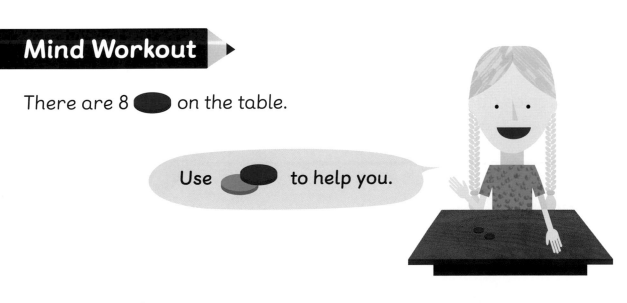

Use ⬤ to help you.

How many ⬤ is Hannah covering with her hand?

Look at the picture.

Make number stories about the number of children.

Make number stories about the number of buckets.

I know how to...

☐ make different number bonds for numbers up to 10.

☐ make number stories.

How many swans are there altogether?

Chapter 3
Addition Within 10

Add by Using Number Bonds

In Focus

How many swans are there altogether?
How can we find out?

Let's Learn

Add by Using Number Bonds

1

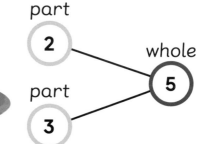

part
2

whole
5

part
3

2	+	3	=	5
part		part		whole

There are 5 swans altogether.

2 + 3 equals 5.

*+ is read as plus.
It means to add.*

We read = as equals.

2 + 3 = 5 is an addition equation.
We read it as two plus three equals five.

2

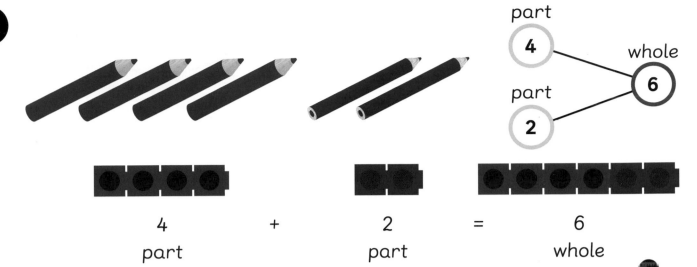

4   +   2   =   6

part   part   whole

There are 6 pencils altogether.

4 plus 2 equals 6.

3

$5 + 0 =$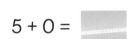

There are oranges altogether.

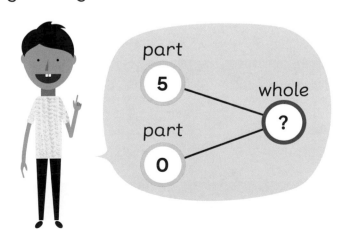

Guided Practice

1 Write the missing numbers.

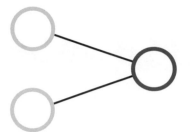

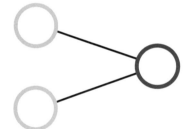 brown horses

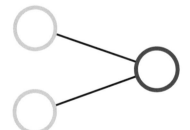 white horse

☐ + ☐ = ☐

There are ☐ horses altogether.

2 Add.

(a)

☐ + ☐ = ☐

(b)

☐ + ☐ = ☐

(c)

☐ + ☐ = ☐

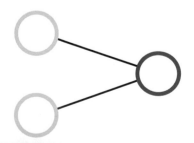

Complete Worksheet 1 – Page 37 - 38

Add by Counting On

In Focus

There are 6 buttons in the box.

How many buttons are there in total?

Let's Learn

Add by Counting On

Count on 3 steps from 6.

1 6 + 3 = ?

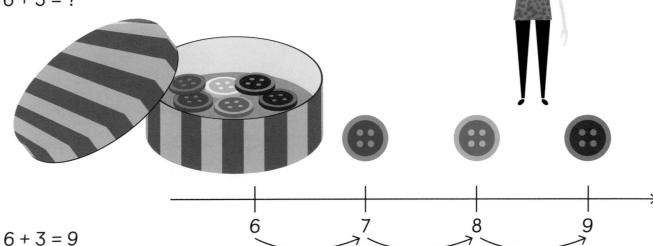

6 + 3 = 9

There are 9 buttons in total.

2 How many eggs are there in total?

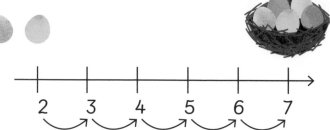

$2 + 5 = 7$

We can also do this.

$5 + 2 = 7$

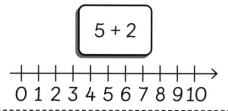

There are ▢ eggs in all.

Why do we count on from the greater number?

Work in pairs.

① Open a 5 + 2 .

② Add by counting on. Use

0 1 2 3 4 5 6 7 8 9 10

to help you.

What you need:

5 + 2

0 1 2 3 4 5 6 7 8 9 10

5

5 + 2

6, 7

5 + 2 = 7

0   1   2   3   4   5   6   7   8   9   10

③ Repeat ① and ② until no cards are left on the table.

Guided Practice

Add by counting on.

(a)

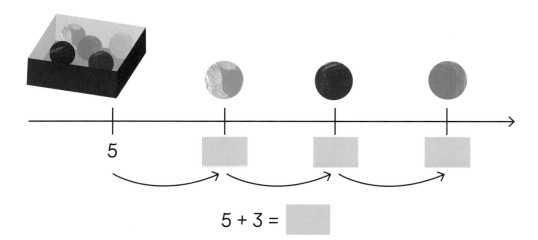

$$5 + 3 = \boxed{}$$

There are ☐ marbles in total.

(b)

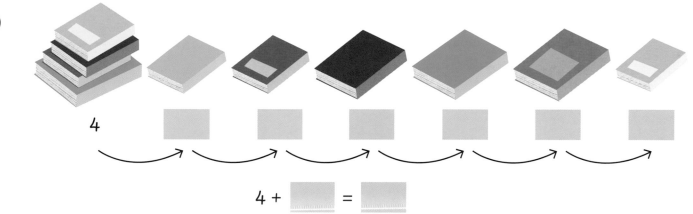

$$4 + \boxed{} = \boxed{}$$

There are ☐ books in all.

(c)

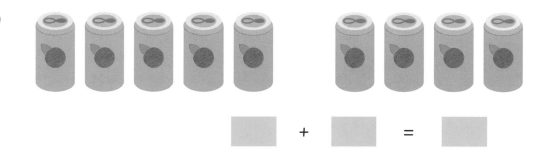

$$\boxed{} + \boxed{} = \boxed{}$$

There are ☐ cans altogether.

Complete Worksheet 2 · Page 39 – 42

Completing Number Sentences

In Focus

How many beans are in the other hand?
How can you tell?

Let's Learn

1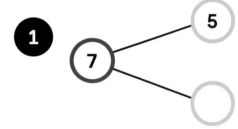

$7 = 5 +$ ▢

I have 7 beans in my hands.

7 is 5 and another number.

2

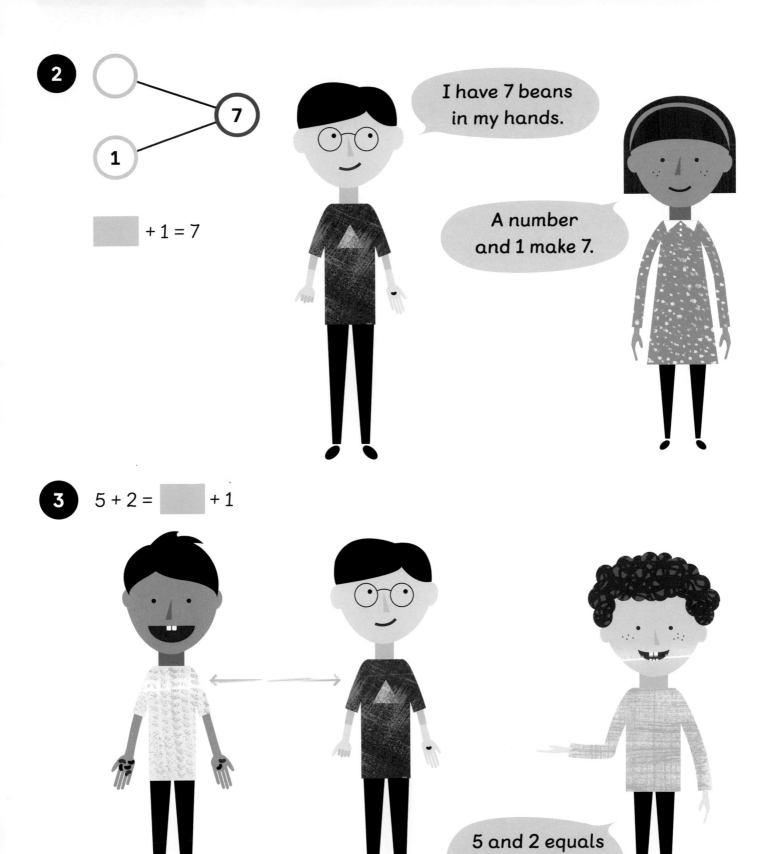

◯
1 ⟶ 7

☐ + 1 = 7

I have 7 beans in my hands.

A number and 1 make 7.

3 5 + 2 = ☐ + 1

5 and 2 equals ☐ and 1.

Complete Worksheet **3** · Page **43 – 44**

Making Addition Stories

What addition stories can you make from the picture?

Let's Learn

1

2 + 3 = 5

5 children are playing on a field.

> 2 children are playing with kites.
> 3 children are playing with a skipping rope.

2

4 children are cycling in front. 2 more children join them.

4 + 2 = ▢

There are ▢ children cycling in all.

Activity Time

Work in pairs.

What you need:

① Make an addition story using  .

② Get your partner to write the addition equation.

There are 6 cubes altogether.

There are 5 green cubes. There is 1 red cube.

5 + 1 = 6

③ Take turns to make addition stories.

How many addition stories can you make?

Guided Practice

Write the missing numbers.

1 There are [ ] goldfish in the bowl.

There are [ ] goldfish in the bag.

[ ] + [ ] = [ ]

There are [ ] goldfish altogether.

2

There are [ ] birds on the branch.

[ ] more birds join them on the branch.

[ ] + [ ] = [ ]

There are [ ] birds on the branch now.

Complete Worksheet 4 · Page **45 – 48**

Solving Picture Problems

In Focus

How many flowers does Lulu have altogether?

Let's Learn

1

   5

   3

How many flowers do you see?

Add 5 and 3. What is the answer?

5 + 3 = 8
Lulu has 8 flowers altogether.

3 children are playing. 4 more children join them.

How many children are there in all?

3 + 4 = [ ]

There are [ ] children in all.

Guided Practice

Solve.

1

How many cupcakes are there altogether?

[ ] + [ ] = [ ]

There are [ ] cupcakes altogether.

2 How many apples does Amira have now?

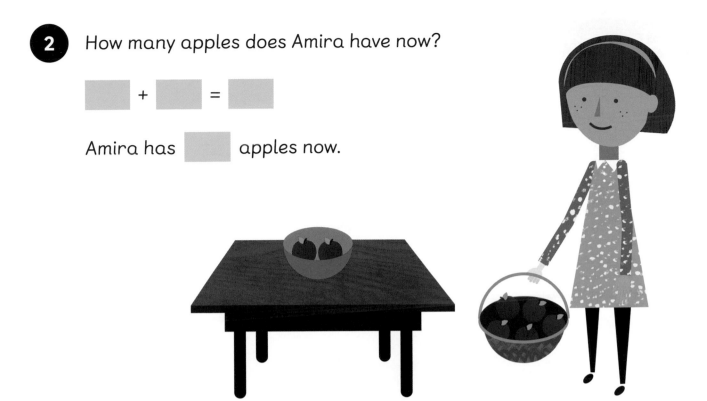

☐ + ☐ = ☐

Amira has ☐ apples now.

▶ Complete Worksheet **5** · Page **49 – 51**

Mind Workout ▶

Make two addition equations.
Use all the cards shown.

+   3   1   +   =

0   6   =   4   6

How many ways can you put the cherries onto the plates?
Show different ways.
Draw pictures.
Write the addition equations.

I know how to...

☐ add by counting.

☐ add by counting on.

☐ make addition stories.

☐ write addition equations.

2 ladybirds fly away.
How many ladybirds are still on the leaf?

Chapter 4
Subtraction Within 10

Subtract by Crossing Out

In Focus

At first, there are 7 ladybirds.

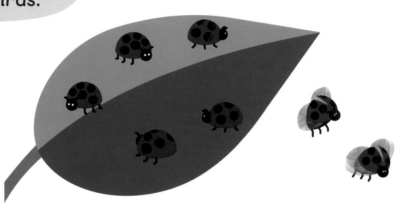

Then, 2 ladybirds fly away.

How many ladybirds are still on the leaf?

Let's Learn

– is read as minus. It means to subtract.

Subtract by Crossing Out

1

$7 - 2 = 5$

5 ladybirds are left.

$7 - 2$ is equal to 5.

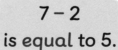 

$7 - 2 = 5$ is a **subtraction equation**.
We read it as seven **minus** two **equals** five.

2

 At first, there are 5 sandwiches.

 Then, I eat 1 sandwich.

How many sandwiches are left?

5 − 1 = 4

There are 4 sandwiches left.

Guided Practice

Subtract by crossing out.

(a)

8 − 5 = ☐

(b)

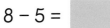

10 − 3 = ☐

(c)

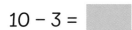

6 − 3 = ☐

Complete Worksheet **1** • Page **57 – 58**

Subtract by Using Number Bonds

In Focus

How many boys do not wear glasses?

There are 4 boys.
3 boys wear glasses.

Let's Learn

Subtract by Using Number Bonds

1

$$4 - 3 = 1$$
whole   part   part

1 boy does not wear glasses.

2

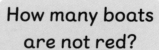

$$7 - 5 = 2$$
2 boats are not red.

How many boats are not red?

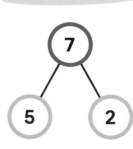

Guided Practice

Subtract using number bonds.

1

$9 - 3 = $ ▢

▢ of the toys are aeroplanes.

There are 9 toys. 3 of the toys are toy robots.

2

$6 - 0 = $ ▢

▢ pelicans are still on the rail.

There are 6 pelicans. None flew away.

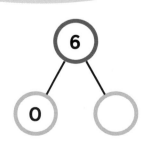

Complete Worksheet **2** – Page **59 - 60**

Subtract by Counting Back

In Focus

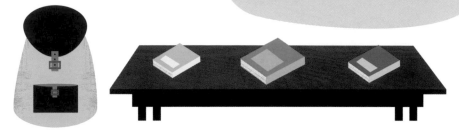

There are 8 books in all.
3 books are on the table.

How many books are there in the bag?

Let's Learn

Subtract by Counting Back

8 – 3 = ?

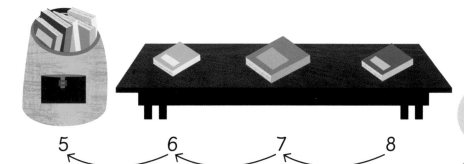

Count back
3 steps from 8.

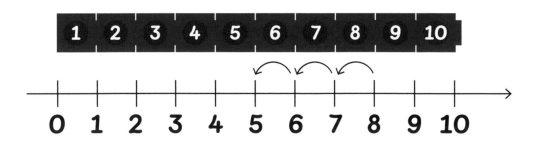

8 – 3 = 5
There are 5 books in the bag.

Play in groups of 3 or 4.

 What you need:

① Show a .

② The other players subtract by counting back.
Example

$5 - 2$

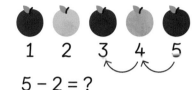

1   2   3   4   5

$5 - 2 = ?$

5, 4, 3
$5 - 2 = 3$

The player who gets a correct answer gets 1 point.

③ The player with the most points wins!

Guided Practice

Subtract by counting back.

There are 9 lemons altogether.

$9 - 2 =$

There are   lemons in the bag.

Complete Worksheet **3** – Page **61 - 62**

Making Subtraction Stories

In Focus

Make subtraction stories.

Let's Learn

1

7 − 1 = 6
6 of the rabbits are white.

2 At first, there were 10 carrots in the ground.

Then, the rabbits pulled 7 carrots out.

10 − 7 = 3
3 carrots remained in the ground.

There are 7 rabbits.
1 rabbit is black.
The rest of the rabbits are white.

How many carrots remained in the ground?

Work in groups of 3 or 4.

What you need:

① Pick a  and make a story.

② Draw a picture to show your story.

Write an equation.

There are 6 worms. 3 worms crawl away.

6 − 3 = 3

3 worms are still in the apple.

③ Show your group's picture to the class.
Tell your subtraction story.

Guided Practice

Write the missing numbers.

(a) There are 10 sheep.

[ ] sheep are black.

10 − [ ] = [ ]

[ ] sheep are white.

(b) There are [ ] sheep.

If [ ] sheep walk away,

[ ] sheep remain.

[ ] − [ ] = [ ]

Complete Worksheet 4 – Page **63 - 66**

Solving Picture Problems

In Focus

How many of the children are girls?

Let's Learn

There are 5 boys.

1

9 – 5 = 4

4 of the children are girls.

Subtract 5 from 9.
What is the answer?

2 At first, there were 9 children on a bus.

3 children got off the bus.

How many children remained on the bus?

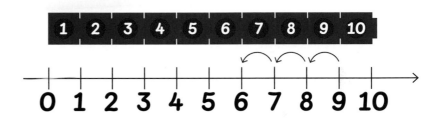

9 – 3 = ▢

▢ children remained on the bus.

Guided Practice

Solve.

1

If 3 balloons fly off, how many balloons remain?

7 – ▢ = ▢

▢ balloons remain.

2 How many eggs are left?

▢ – ▢ = ▢

 has ▢ eggs.

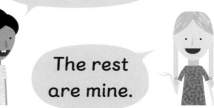

5 eggs are mine.

The rest are mine.

Complete Worksheet **5** – Page **67 - 68**

Addition and Subtraction

In Focus

Write addition and subtraction equations.

There are 7 apples. 5 apples are red and 2 apples are green.

Let's Learn

How many apples are there altogether?

| 5 + 2 = 7 | or | 2 + 5 = 7 |

How many apples are red?

| 7 − 2 = 5 |

How many apples are green?

| 7 − 5 = 2 |

part   part

5   2

7

whole

These are addition and subtraction equations.
They make up a **family of addition and subtraction facts.**

Make a family of addition and subtraction facts.

[ ] + [ ] = [ ]   [ ] − [ ] = [ ]

[ ] + [ ] = [ ]   [ ] − [ ] = [ ]

Complete Worksheet 6 – Page 69 - 71

Mind Workout

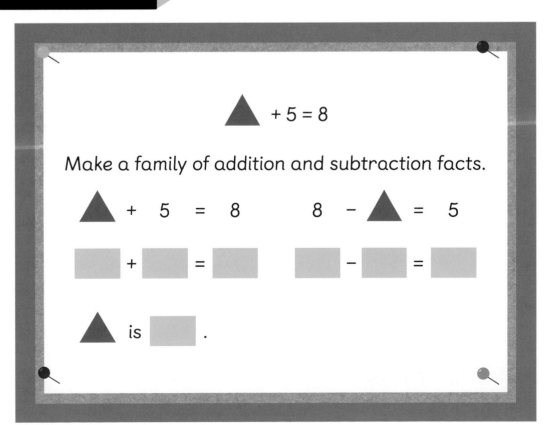

△ + 5 = 8

Make a family of addition and subtraction facts.

△ + 5 = 8   8 − △ = 5

[ ] + [ ] = [ ]   [ ] − [ ] = [ ]

△ is [ ] .

Look at the picture.

Make a subtraction story.

Make a family of addition and subtraction facts for the story.

Self Check

I know how to...

☐ subtract by crossing out.

☐ subtract using number bonds.

☐ subtract by counting back.

☐ make subtraction stories.

☐ write subtraction equations.

☐ make a family of addition and subtraction facts.

Who is first in the race?

Chapter 5
Positions

Naming Positions

In Focus

Can you name the position of each runner in the race?

Let's Learn

1

first   second   third   fourth   fifth

2

Hannah is sixth in the race.

Sam finishes the race after Hannah.

Sam is seventh in the race.

Emma finishes the race after Sam and before Holly.
Emma is eighth.
Holly is ninth.

Holly finishes the race before Amira.
Amira is tenth.

Is Amira last in the race?

Make a group of 10.

What you need:

[1st] [3rd] [5th]

① Have a race.

② Pick the correct position cards to show the position of each person in the race.

Guided Practice

1

☐ is first in the race.

☐ is second in the race.

 is ☐ in the race.

2 Who finished the race after Amira?

Ravi finished the race after Charles.

Ravi was ☐ in the race.

Ruby finished the race before Sam but after Ravi.

Ruby was ☐ .

Sam was ☐ .

Amira

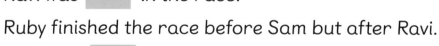
Complete Worksheet **1** – Page **85 - 87**

Naming Positions in Queues

In Focus

Emma   Ravi   Amira   Sam   Ruby

Holly   Charles   Hannah   Lulu   Elliott

Can you name the position of each person in the queue?

Let's Learn

2nd second   4th fourth   6th sixth   8th eighth   10th tenth

1st first   3rd third   5th fifth   7th seventh   9th ninth

Hannah is after Ravi.

Sam is before Elliott.

Lulu is between Amira and Sam.

1 There are 5 children in the queue.
   What is the position of each child in the queue?

Sam   Lulu   Hannah   Ravi   Emma

			second	
			2nd	

(a) ____ is first in the queue.

(b) Lulu is ____ in the queue.

(c) Ravi is ____ in the queue.

(d) ____ is after Lulu.

(e) Hannah is between ____ and ____ .

(f) ____ is last in the queue.

Complete Worksheet 2 – Page 88 - 89

Naming Left and Right Positions

In Focus

left

  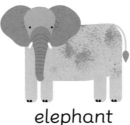 

right

giraffe   monkey   zebra   elephant   tiger

Can you name the position of each animal from the left?
Can you do the same from the right?

Let's Learn

We can name the position of each animal starting from the left or the right.

1. The is first from the **left**.

   The is second from the left.

   The  is fifth from the **right**.
   It is also **last** from the right.

   The  is third from the left.
   It is also third from the right.

What is the position of the from the right?

   The is **next to** the . It is also next to the .

   The is **between** the and the .

2

Emma

Lulu

Ravi

Lulu is in the first row.
She is second from the left.
She is also fifth from the right.

Emma is in the second row.
She is fifth from the left.
She is also first from the right.

Can you name Ravi's position?

Activity Time

Work in pairs.

What you need:

Your family photograph

① Look at the 📷.

② Tell your partner your position in the 📷.

    (a) I am in the ▢ row.

    (b) I am ▢ from the left.

    (c) I am ▢ from the right.

    (d) I am next to ▢ .

③ Read the sentences aloud to describe your position.

④ Ask your partner to check your answers.

left   right

Holly   Ravi   Ruby   Lulu   Amira   Emma   Sam   Elliott

What is the position of each child?

(a) _____ is fourth from the left.

(b) _____ is next to Elliott.

(c) _____ is between Holly and Ruby.

(d) Amira is _____ from the right. She is also _____ from the left.

Complete Worksheet 3 – Page 90 - 91 ▶

Mind Workout ▶

Hannah wants to decorate a cake.
Name the pictures from first to sixth to show the correct order.

The toys are mixed up.

Read the sentences below.

The teddy bear is first from the right.
The teddy bear is next to the car.
The dinosaur is between the rubber duck and the car.

Draw the toys in the correct positions.

I know how to...

☐ name positions in a race and in a queue.

☐ name positions from the left and from the right.

☐ use words such as before, after, next to, last and between to name positions.

Self Check

Is it easier to count the number of eggs or strawberries?

Chapter 6
Numbers to 20

Counting to 20

In Focus

Count on from 10.

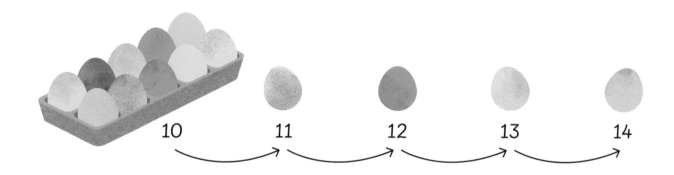

10   11   12   13   14

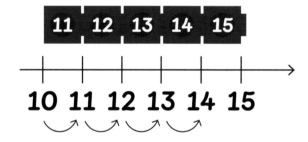

| 11 | 12 | 13 | 14 | 15 |

10 11 12 13 14 15

Why is it easier to count on from 10?

There are 14 eggs.

1 How many strawberries are there?

Make 10 and count on.

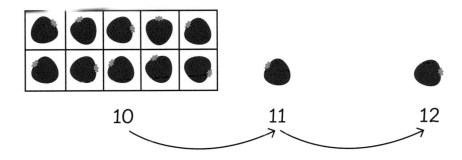

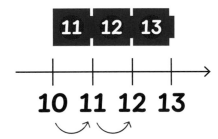

10 and 2 make 12.

10 + 2 = 12

There are 12 strawberries.

2 Count on from 10.

11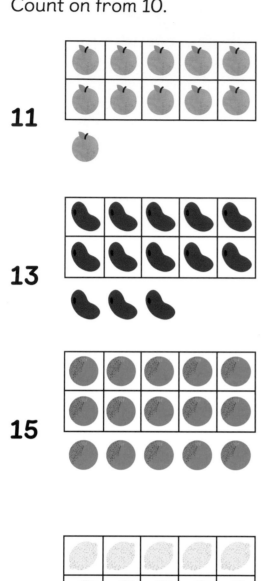

12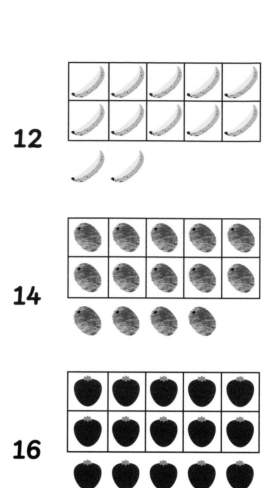

13

14

15

16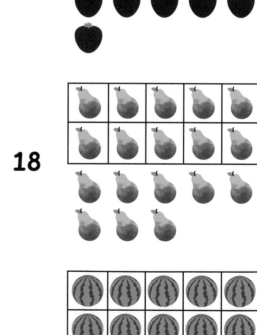

17

18

19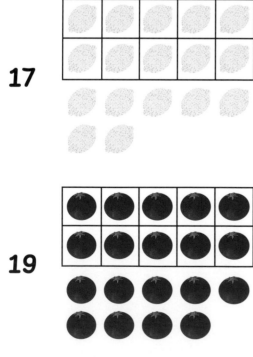

20

Work in pairs.

What you need:

① Collect three sets of ⬤.

② For each set, make 10 and count on.
Get your partner to write the addition equation.

10, 11, 12

$10 + 2 = 12$

③ Take turns to count and write the addition equation.

Guided Practice

Count out 10.
Then count on from 10.

10 and 9 make ☐ .

$10 + 9 =$ ☐

Complete Worksheet 1 – Page 95 – 98

Writing to 20

In Focus

Count the flowers.
How do we write the number in words?

Let's Learn

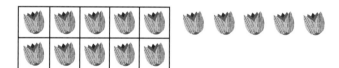

11   eleven

12   twelve

13   thirteen

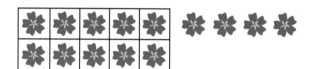

14   fourteen

15   fifteen

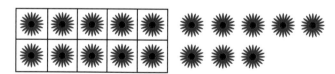

16   sixteen

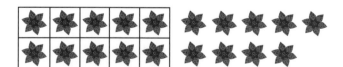

17   seventeen

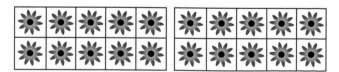

18   eighteen

19   nineteen

20   twenty

Play in groups of 3.

What you need:

① Put the cards face down on the table.

② Take turns to pick a [20] and a [twenty].
If they match, keep them.
If they do not match, turn them back over.

The cards match!

③ The player with the most cards wins!

Guided Practice

Make 10 and count.
Write in numbers and in words.

(a)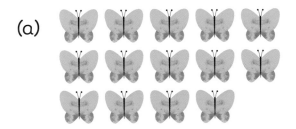

(b)

Complete Worksheet **2** – Page **99 – 102**

Comparing Numbers

In Focus

Which bus stop has more children?

Bus Stop A
13 children

Bus Stop B
11 children

Bus Stop A has more children than Bus Stop B.
Bus Stop B has fewer children than Bus Stop A.

Activity Time

Work in pairs.

What you need:

① Compare two groups of .
  (a) Which group has more?
  (b) Which group has fewer?

There are 15 counters in Group A.
There are 12 counters in Group B.

Group A has more counters than Group B.
Group B has fewer counters than Group A.

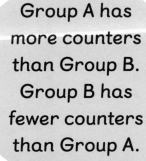

② Make another two groups with different numbers of .
  Compare the two groups.

1 Compare using **more** or **fewer**.

Group A
12 toy soldiers

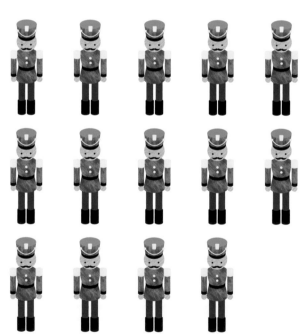

Group B
14 toy soldiers

(a)   Group A has [____] toy soldiers than Group B.

(b)   Group B has [____] toy soldiers than Group A.

2 Count and compare.

Group C
▢ ribbons

Group D
▢ ribbons

(a) Group C has [   ] ribbons than Group D.

(b) Group D has [   ] ribbons than Group C.

Complete Worksheet 3 – Page 103 - 106 ▶

Ordering Numbers

In Focus

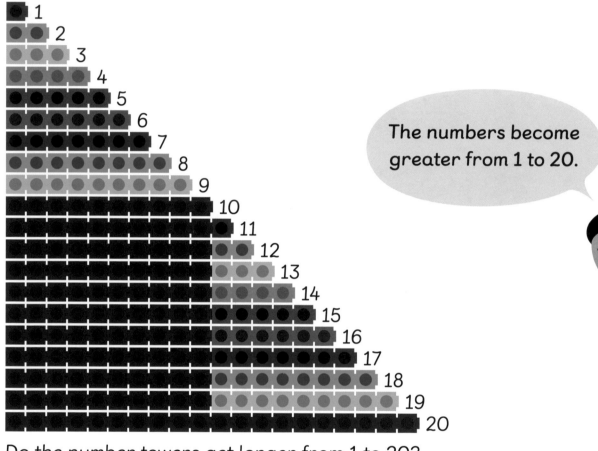

1
2
3
4
5
6
7
8
9
10
11
12
13
14
15
16
17
18
19
20

The numbers become greater from 1 to 20.

Do the number towers get longer from 1 to 20?

Let's Learn

1 Compare 11 and 15.

11

15

15 is more than 11.

11 is less than 15.

2 Compare 16, 13 and 17.

16

13

17

17 is more than 13.
17 is more than 16.
17 is the greatest.

13 is less than 16.
13 is less than 17.
13 is the smallest.

Arrange the numbers in order.
Start with the greatest.

17,   **16,**   **13**

greatest $\longrightarrow$ smallest

We can also start with the smallest.

13,   **16,**   **17**

smallest $\longrightarrow$ greatest

Play in groups of 3 to 4.

 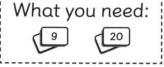
① Take a card each.
Compare the numbers.

8 is less than 14.
8 is less than 11.
8 is the smallest.

14 is the greatest.

② Arrange the numbers in order.
Start with the smallest.

③ The player with the greatest number keeps the cards.

④ After 5 rounds, the player with the most cards wins!

Guided Practice

1 Which is less, 18 or 10?

2 Compare 11, 19 and 13.

   (a)   The greatest number is   .

   (b)   Arrange the numbers in order.
          Start with the smallest.

         ,   ,

3 Arrange 9, 19 and 14 in order.
Start with the greatest.

       ,   ,

Complete Worksheet 4 – Page **107 – 110**

Number Patterns

In Focus

Use square tiles to show numbers from 8 to 11.

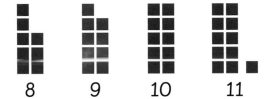

8   9   10   11

What comes next?

Let's Learn

1

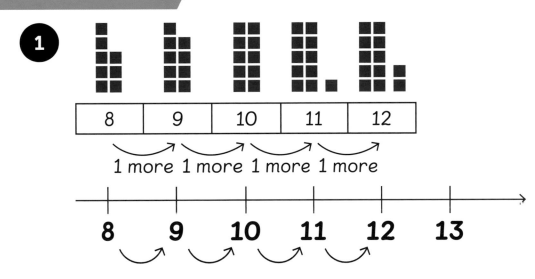

9 is 1 more than 8.
10 is 1 more than 9.
11 is 1 more than 10.

What is 1 more than 11?
12 is 1 more than 11.

8, 9, 10, 11, 12 is a **number pattern**.

Each number is 1 more than the number before.

2

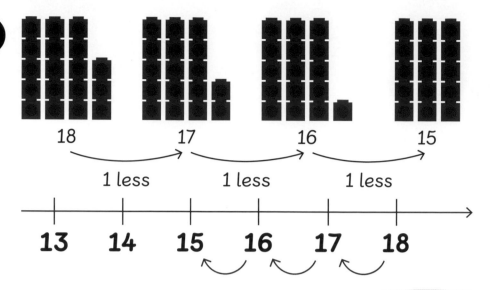

18   17   16   15

1 less   1 less   1 less

13   14   15   16   17   18

17 is 1 less than 18.
16 is 1 less than 17.
15 is 1 less than 16.

Each number is 1 less than the number before.

What is 1 less than 15?
The number pattern is 18, 17, 16, 15, .

Activity Time

Work in pairs.

What you need:

① Use to make a pattern.

② Get your partner to tell you what number comes next in the pattern.

13 is 1 more than 12.
14 is 1 more than 13.
The next number is 14.

What comes next?

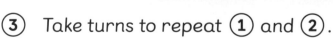

③ Take turns to repeat ① and ②.

Find the missing numbers.
Use ▓ to help you.

(a) ▢ is 1 more than 6.

(b) ▢ is 1 less than 10.

(c) ▢ is 1 more than 19.

(d) ▢ is 1 less than 11.

 Complete the number patterns.

(a) 6, 7, 8, 9, ▢ , 11

(b) 12, 13, 14, 15, ▢ , ▢ , 18

(c) 12, 11, 10, 9, ▢ , ▢ , 6

(d) ▢ , 19, 18, 17, ▢ , ▢ , 14

Complete Worksheet 5 – Page 111 – 114

Mind Workout

Use the numbers below to make two number patterns.
You can use each number only once.

| 9 | 15 | 16 | 14 | 12 | 10 |

Pattern 1: ▢ , ▢ , 11, ▢

Pattern 2: ▢ , ▢ , ▢ , 13

Look at the picture.

Hannah: I have 20 ribbons.

Lulu: I have 12 ribbons.

Amira: I have 17 ribbons.

Write two sentences to compare the number of ribbons that the girls have.

Example

Amira has more ribbons than Lulu.

Self Check

I know how to...

☐ count to 20.

☐ read and write numbers from 11 to 20.

☐ compare and order numbers within 20.

☐ complete number patterns.

How many buns are there altogether?

Chapter 7
Addition and Subtraction Within 20

Add by Counting On

In Focus

8

$8 + 3 = ?$

3

What are the different ways to add?

Let's Learn

Add by Counting On

Count on 3 steps from 8.

1

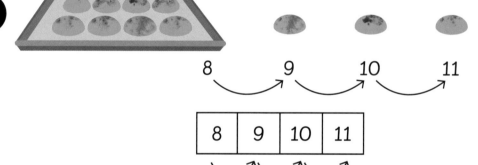

$$8 \quad 9 \quad 10 \quad 11$$

8	9	10	11

$8 + 3 = 11$

There are 11 buns altogether.

2 $11 + 3 = ?$

Why do we count on from 11?

11	12	13	14

$11 + 3 = 14$

Play in groups of 2 to 3.

What you need:

10	11	12	13	14	15

① Roll a and a .

② Add the two numbers by counting on.

③ Find the number on your

10	11	12	13	14	15

Put a on the number. You lose a turn if the number is less than 10.

9, 10, 11
9 + 2 = 11

④ Take turns to repeat ① to ③.

⑤ The first player to cover all the numbers wins!

Guided Practice

Add by counting on.

5	6	7	8	9	10	11	12	13	14	15	16	17	18	19	20

(a) 7 + 4 =

(b) 2 + 9 =

(c) 12 + 2 =

(d) 4 + 15 =

Complete Worksheet 1 – Page 119 - 120

Add by Making 10

In Focus

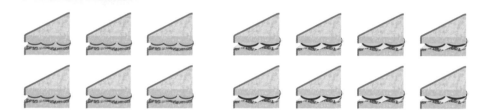

How many sandwiches are there?

Let's Learn

Add by Making 10

1 6 + 8 = ?

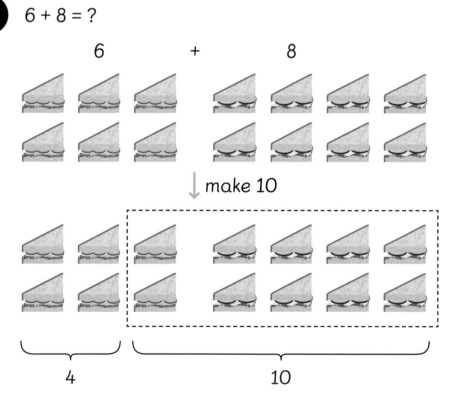

6   +   8

↓ make 10

4   10

6 + 8 = 14
There are 14 sandwiches.

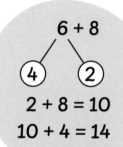

6 + 8

4   2

2 + 8 = 10
10 + 4 = 14

2 9 + 3 = ?

Use square tiles to show
the two numbers.

9   +   3

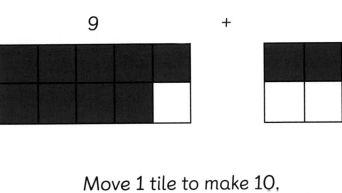

Move 1 tile to make 10.

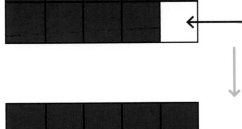

10   2

9 + 3 = 12

9 + 3

9 + 1 = 10
10 + 2 = 12

Is 9 + 3 the same as 3 + 9?
Why?

Work in pairs.

What you need:

① Take turns to pick two  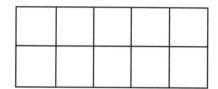.

② Put ▪ on each grid to show each number.

③ Add the two numbers.
Make 10 to add if needed.

Example

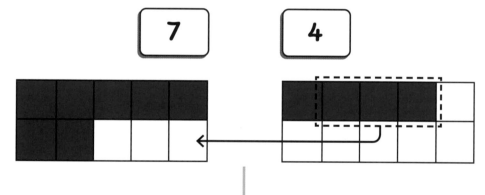

7   4

④ Check each other's answers.

Add by making 10.

(a)

6 + 4 = ▢

4 + 6 = ▢

(b)

9 + 4 = ▢

4 + 9 = ▢

Complete Worksheet **2** – Page **121 - 124**

Add by Adding Ones

In Focus

How many candles are there altogether?

Let's Learn

Add Ones

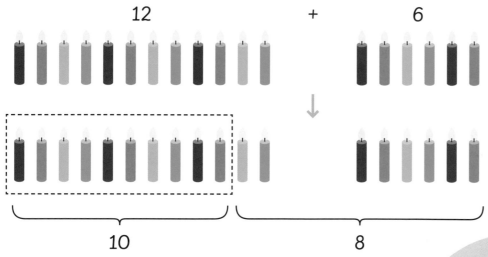

12 + 6 = 18

There are 18 candles altogether.

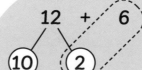
2 + 6 = 8
10 + 8 = 18

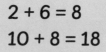

Play in groups of 3 to 4.

What you need:

15 (10 – 15)   4 (1 – 4)

(1) Place the [15] and [4] face down on the table.

(2) Turn over two cards.
Add the two numbers shown.

Example

[15]   [4]

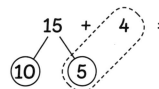

15 + 4 = 19

(10) (5)

The first player to get the correct answer keeps the cards.

(3) The player with the most cards wins!

Guided Practice

Add.

(a) 13 + 4 = [ ]

◯ ◯

(b) 4 + 13 = [ ]

◯ ◯

Complete Worksheet 3 – Page 125 - 127

Subtract by Counting Back

In Focus

$15 - 3 = ?$

What are the different ways to subtract?

Let's Learn

Subtract by Counting Back

Count back 3 steps from 15.

Subtract 3 from 15.

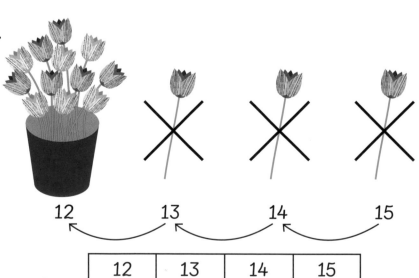

$15 - 3 = 12$

There are 12 flowers left.

Play in groups of 2 to 4.

What you need:

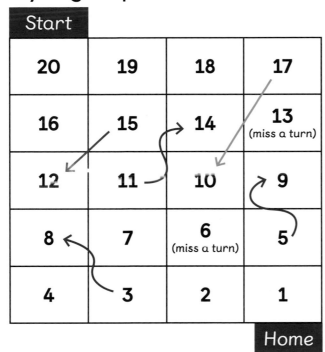

① Choose a ⬤ and put it on 20.

② Take turns to roll the 🎲 to get a number.

③ Subtract by counting back from where your ⬤ is.

④ The first player to reach Home wins!

Guided Practice

Subtract by counting back.

11	12	13	14	15	16	17	18	19	20

(a) 15 − 2 =

(b) 17 − 3 =

Complete Worksheet 4 – Page 128 – 129

Subtract by Subtracting Ones

In Focus

4 flowers wither and die.
How many flowers are left?

Let's Learn

Subtract Ones

1 16 − 4 = ?

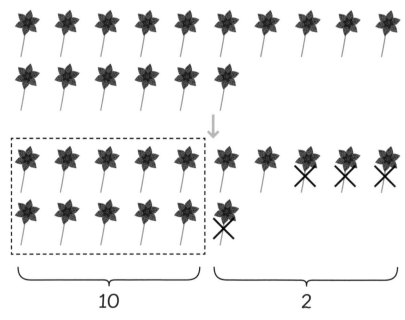

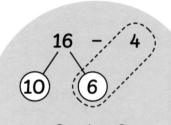

6 − 4 = 2
10 + 2 = 12

16 − 4 = 12
There are 12 flowers left.

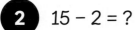 **2** 15 − 2 = ?

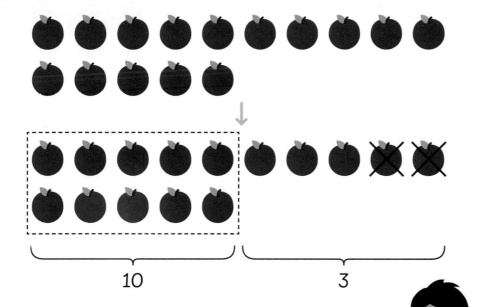

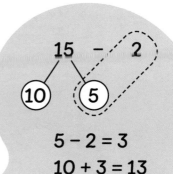

15 − 2
10   5
5 − 2 = 3
10 + 3 = 13

15 − 2 = 13
There are 13 apples left.

Guided Practice

Subtract.

(a) 17 − 5 = ⬜

○ ○

(b) 17 − 7 = ⬜

○ ○

Complete Worksheet **5** – Page **130 – 132**

Subtract from 10

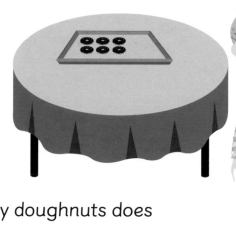

I will give you 8 doughnuts.

How many doughnuts does Sam have left?

Let's Learn

Subtract from 10

$14 - 8 = ?$

Put 10 in a box ↓

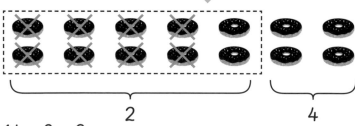

2   4

$14 - 8 = 6$

Sam has 6 doughnuts left.

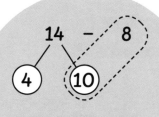

$14 - 8$

4   10

$10 - 8 = 2$

$4 + 2 = 6$

Play in groups of 3 to 4.

① Pick up a 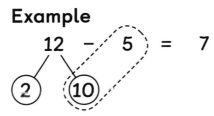 and a 20 .
Subtract the smaller number from the greater number.

Example

12 – 5 = 7

② 10

Subtract 5 from 10.

② The player with the correct answer keeps the cards.

③ The player with the most cards wins!

Guided Practice

1 Subtract from 10.

(a)

15 – 7 =

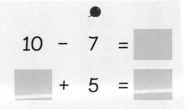

$10 - 7 = \boxed{}$

$\boxed{} + 5 = \boxed{}$

(b)

13 – 9 =

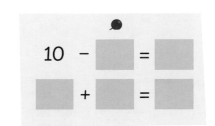

$10 - \boxed{} = \boxed{}$

$\boxed{} + \boxed{} = \boxed{}$

2 Subtract.

(a)   13 – 5 =

(b)   17 – 9 =

Complete Worksheet 6 – Page 133 – 135

Addition and Subtraction Facts

In Focus

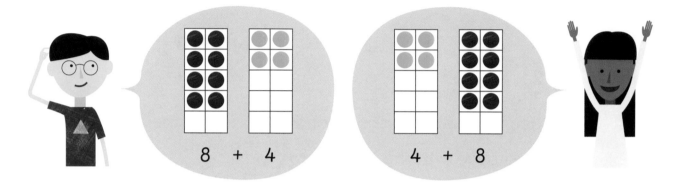

8 + 4   4 + 8

Is 8 + 4 the same as 4 + 8?

Let's Learn

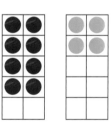

1

8   +   4   =   10   +   2
                =   12

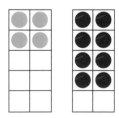

4   +   8   =   10   +   2
                =   12

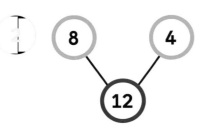

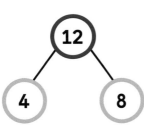

8 + 4 = 12
4 + 8 = 12

This is a family of addition and subtraction facts.

12 − 8 = 4
12 − 4 = 8

Guided Practice

(1) 7 + 4 = 11

11 − 7 =

11 − 4 =

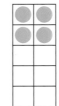

2 7 + 4 = 11

7 + 5 =

8 + 4 =

7 + 4 = 11
8 + 5 =

Complete Worksheet 7 – Page 136 – 138

Mind Workout

Complete the equations.

(a) 14 + ⬚ = 19

(b) 17 − ⬚ = 6

(c) ⬚ + 9 = 15

(d) ⬚ − 9 = 8

Add.

Do you know your doubles facts?

(a) 1 + 1 = ☐

(b) 2 + 2 = ☐

(c) 3 + 3 = ☐

(d) 4 + 4 = ☐

(e) 5 + 5 = ☐

(f) 6 + 6 = ☐

(g) 7 + 7 = ☐

(h) 8 + 8 = ☐

(i) 9 + 9 = ☐

(j) 10 + 10 = ☐

How can you use 7 + 7 to find 7 + 8 and 7 + 6?

Self Check

I know how to...

☐ add by counting on.

☐ add by making 10.

☐ add by adding ones.

☐ subtract by counting back.

☐ subtract by subtracting ones.

☐ subtract by subtracting from 10.

☐ make a family of addition and subtraction facts.

What shapes can you see?

Chapter 8
Shapes and Patterns

Recognising Solids

In Focus

What shapes can you see?

Let's Learn

1 These are **spheres**.

2 These are **cubes**.

3 These are **cuboids**.

4 These are **pyramids**.

These are not pyramids.

Work in groups.

① Look for solids (cubes, cuboids, pyramids and spheres) around you.

② Name them.

This is a cuboid.

Guided Practice

These are drawings of solids. Name the solids.

| cube | cuboid | pyramid | sphere |

Complete Worksheet 1 – Page 141 – 142

Recognising Shapes

In Focus

Can you name the shapes in the picture?

Let's Learn

1 These are **squares**.

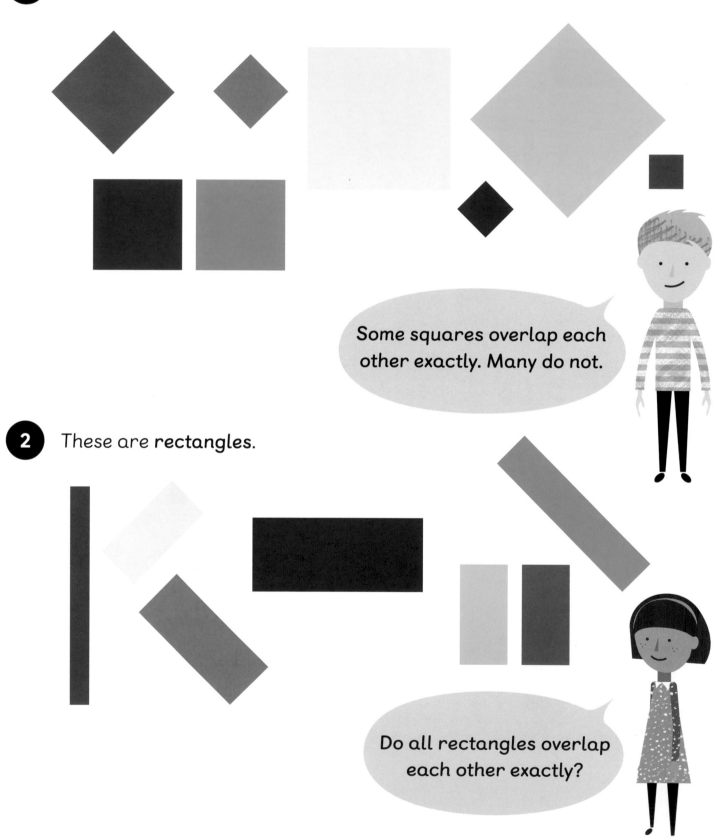

Some squares overlap each other exactly. Many do not.

2 These are **rectangles**.

Do all rectangles overlap each other exactly?

3 These are **triangles**.

4 These are **circles**.

Work in pairs.

What you need:

① Take turns to pick up one object.
Name and trace one shape you see.

The Rubik's cube is a cube.

The Rubik's cube has squares.

Which object has more than one shape?

② Look for objects around you that have squares, rectangles, triangles or circles.

Guided Practice

1 Which shapes are triangles?

2 Which shapes are rectangles?

3 Which shapes are squares?

4 Which shapes are circles?

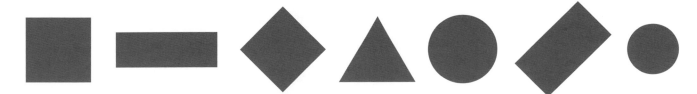

Complete Worksheet **2** – Page **143 – 145**

Grouping Shapes

In Focus

How can we group the shapes?

We can group them by **shape**.

Let's Learn

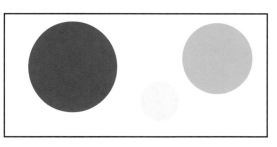

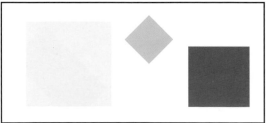
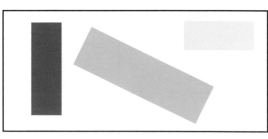

2

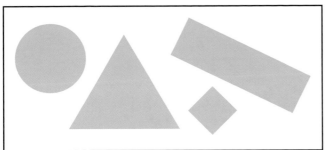

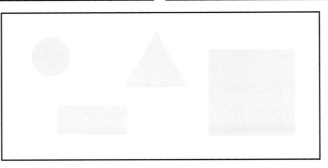

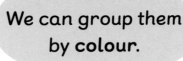

We can group them by **colour.**

3

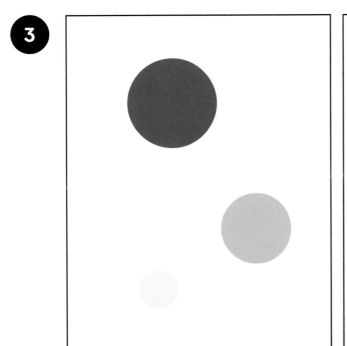

How are we grouping these shapes?

Work in pairs.

What you need:

① Put the  into groups by shape or colour.

② Ask your partner to say how you grouped the shapes.

③ Take turns to sort the  into different groups.

The shapes are grouped by **colour.**

Guided Practice

How are the shapes grouped?

(a)

The shapes are grouped by _____ .

(b)

The shapes are grouped by _____ .

(c)

The shapes are grouped by _____ .

Complete Worksheet **3** – Page **146 - 147**

Making Patterns

In Focus

How are the shapes arranged on the birthday card?

Let's Learn

1

There is a change in colour.

| yellow, red | , | yellow, red | , ...

2

There is a change in size.

| big, small | , | big, small | , ...

These are **patterns**. What comes next in each pattern?

3

There is a change in size and shape.

   big circle, small square , 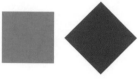 big circle, small square , ...

4

What is the pattern?
What comes next in the pattern?

Activity Time

Work in groups of 3 to 4.

Do this activity on a computer.

① Use the shapes tool to draw the shapes above.

② Choose 2 shapes and make a pattern.

③ Print out your pattern.

④ Ask another group to describe your pattern and guess what comes next.

Guided Practice

Pick a shape to complete each pattern.

(a)

(b)

Why did you pick those shapes?

Complete Worksheet 4 – Page **148 - 149**

Mind Workout

Each day, Ravi draws a picture to form a pattern.

Draw the picture that Ravi draws on Friday.

What is the rule that Ravi uses to make the pattern?

   ?

Monday   Tuesday   Wednesday   Thursday   Friday   Saturday   Sunday

Maths Journal

Cut a square, rectangle, triangle and circle into 2 pieces.

Mix the pieces up.

Put the pieces back together to make a square, rectangle, triangle, and circle.

Paste them in your journal. Name the shapes you make.

I know how to...

☐ name solids and shapes.

☐ look for shapes in solids.

☐ group shapes.

☐ make and complete patterns with shapes.

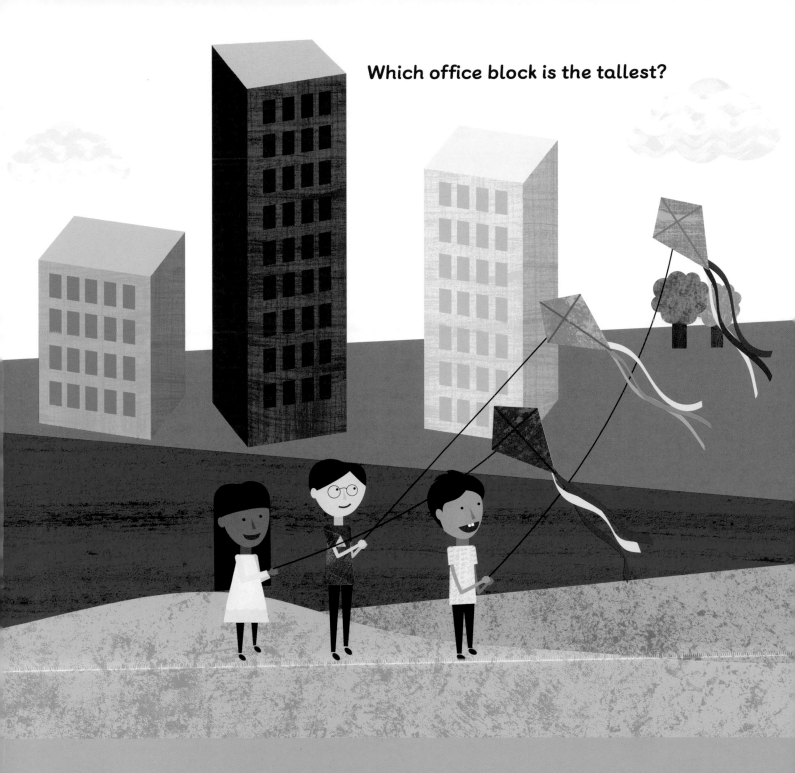

Which office block is the tallest?

Chapter 9
Length and Height

Comparing Height and Length

In Focus

How can we compare the office blocks?

Let's Learn

1 The  is **tall**. It is **taller** than the yellow office block.

The is **short**. It is **shorter** than the yellow office block.

The is the **tallest**. The is the **shortest**.

We can arrange the office blocks from tallest to shortest.

tallest ⟶ shortest

We only use tallest or shortest when comparing the height of 3 or more objects.

2

This piece of rope is short.

This rope is long.

starting line

← green

← orange

← blue

← red

We can compare length using a starting line.

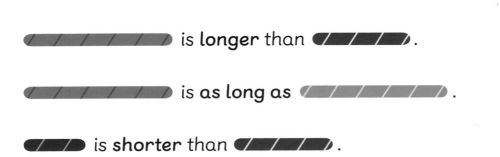

is **longer** than ⬛⬛⬛.

is **as long as** ▬▬▬▬▬▬.

is **shorter** than ▬▬▬.

Work in pairs.

What you need:

① Cut out a piece of 〜.

② Cut out a piece of 〜 that is longer than the 〜.

③ Cut out a piece of 〜 that is shorter than the 〜.

④ Talk to your partner about the different lengths of the 3 pieces of paper.

> Which is the longest piece?

Guided Practice

Look for objects around the classroom.
Compare using **taller**, **longer** or **shorter**.

(a) The teacher's table is ▒▒▒▒▒▒ than my table.

(b) My ruler is ▒▒▒▒▒▒ than my rubber.

(c) My pen is ▒▒▒▒▒▒ than my pencil.

(d) I am ▒▒▒▒▒▒ than my teacher.

(e) I am ▒▒▒▒▒▒ than my friend.

> When do you use taller or longer to describe an object?

Complete Worksheet 1 – Page 153 – 156

Measuring Length Using Things

In Focus

Which is longer, the pencil or the crayon?

Let's Learn

We can use 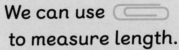 to measure length.

What other things can we use to measure length?

The pencil is about 6 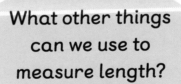 long.
The crayon is about 5 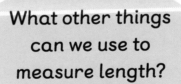 long.

The pencil is longer than the crayon.
The crayon is shorter than the pencil.

Activity Time

Work in pairs.

What you need:

(1) Look at objects around you.

(2) Guess the length of each object.

(3) Use to measure the length.

Example

Your pencil case 	I guess my pencil case is about ___ long.
	My pencil case is about ___ long.

Guided Practice

How tall are 😊 and 😊 ?

I am about ___ sticks tall.

I am about ___ tall.

Complete Worksheet 2 – Page 157 – 160

Measuring Height and Length Using Body Parts

In Focus

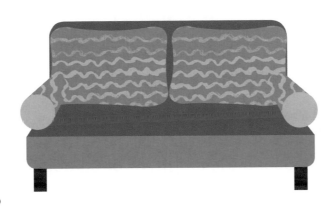

How long is the sofa?
Which part of our body can we use to find out?

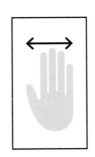

Let's Learn

We can use parts of our body to measure length.

Is it also

10  long?

Why not?

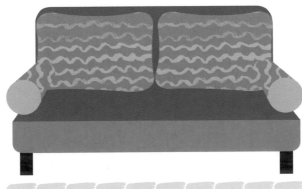

The sofa is about 10 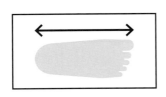 long.
We can also say that the length of the sofa is about 10 units.

Work in pairs.

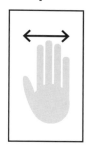 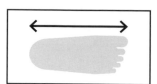

① Pick a part of the body.

② Use it to measure the length of each object.

③ Record the length of each object.

Object		
desk		
pencil case		
whiteboard		

 is as tall as 2 .

Its height is also 5 .

Is this possible?

1 Count.

(a)   The carpet is about ▢ 🦶 long.

(b)   The length of the carpet is about ▢ units.

2 Use 🖐 to measure the length of your desk.

(a)   My desk is about ▢ 🖐 long.

(b)   The length of my desk is about ▢ units.

3 Use 🖐 to measure the height of your desk.

The height of my desk is about ▢ units.

🖐 = 1 unit

Complete Worksheet **3** – Page **161**

Measuring Height and Length Using a Ruler

In Focus

How tall is the toy soldier?
How long is the train?

Let's Learn

 is about 8 centimetres tall.

 is about 10 centimetres long.

This is 1 centimetre long.

Work in pairs.

(1) Make your own ruler.

What you need:

Example

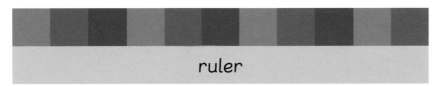

ruler

(2) Use your ruler to measure how long these lines are.

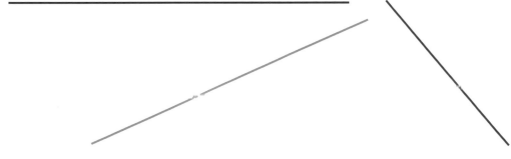

(3) Use your ruler to measure the height and length of different objects in the classroom.

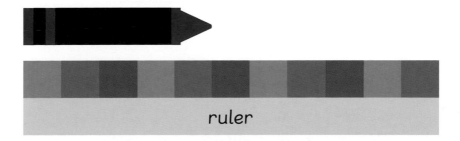

ruler

Guided Practice

The pictures show four objects.

Use [   ] to measure the length of the objects.

(a)

is about [   ] centimetres long.

(b)

is about [   ] centimetres long.

(c)

is about [   ] centimetres long.

(d)

is about [   ] centimetres long.

Complete Worksheet 4 – Page 162 - 163

Mind Workout

Compare the length of the objects.

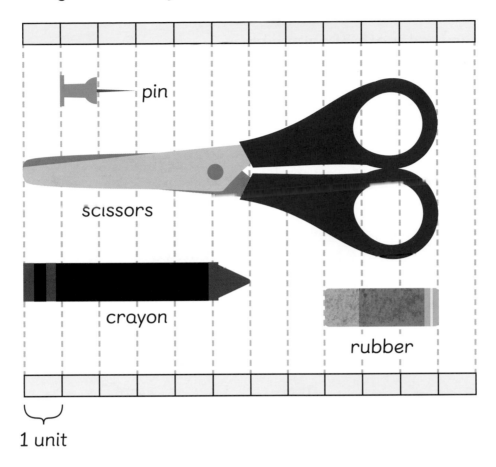

1 unit

(a)   The [   ] is shorter than the rubber.

(b)   The [   ] is shortest.

(c)

The length of the colouring pencil is about [   ] units.

Emma has a red ribbon and a blue ribbon.

She measures the length of each ribbon.

The red ribbon is about 7 paper clips long.

The blue ribbon is about 4 ice lolly sticks long.

I use more paper clips than ice lolly sticks.
So, the red ribbon is longer than the blue ribbon.

Is Emma correct?

Why?

I know how to...

☐ compare the length of objects.

☐ measure the length of objects.

Self Check